Cool Crafts with
Cardboard

Jane Yates

WINDMILL
BOOKS

Published in 2018 by **Windmill Books**,
an Imprint of Rosen Publishing
29 East 21st Street, New York, NY 10010

Developed and produced for Rosen by BlueApple*Works* Inc.

Creative Director: Melissa McClellan
Managing Editor for BlueApple*Works*: Melissa McClellan
Designer: T.J. Choleva
Photo Research: Jane Reid
Editor: Marcia Abramson
Craft Artisans: Janet Kompare-Fritz (p.18); Jane Yates (p. 10, 12, 14, 16, 20, 22, 24, 26); Jerrie McClellan (p. 8, 28)

Photo Credits: cover upper right, title page AllaR15/Shutterstock.com; cover top banner, title page autsawin uttisin/
Shutterstock.com; background paper cover, TOC Becky Starsmore/Shutterstock.com; cover bottom banner, title
page Mega Pixel/Shutterstock.com; TOC, page backgrounds Ipek Morel/Shutterstock.com; p. 4 top Ermolaevamariya/
Dreamstime.com; p. 4 middle Richard Thomas/Dreamstime.com; p. 4 bottom jocic/Shutterstock.com; p. 5 top to
bottom and left to right: Photka/Dreamstime.com; kontur-vid/Shutterstock.com; Sappachoats/Shutterstock.com;
Freedom_Studio/Shutterstock.com; Crackerclips/Dreamstime.com; Jirk4/Dreamstime.com; paranut/Shutterstock.com;
Photo Melon/Shutterstock.com; Onur Ersin/Dreamstime.com; Jerryb8/Dreamstime.com; GeniusKp/Shutterstock.com;
Christian Bertrand/Dreamstime.com; Lyudmila Suvorova/Shutterstock.com; NuDesign.co/Shutterstock.com; Artur
Synenko/Shutterstock.com; p. 8 right Ivan Kulikov/Shutterstock.com; p. 9 bottom left Africa Studio/Shutterstock.com;
p. 14 right Vadim.Petrov/Shutterstock.com; p. 18 right AdamBoor/Shutterstock.com; p. 20 djhalcyonic/Shutterstock.
com; p. 22 bottom Alex Kosev/Shutterstock.com; p. 22 right Syda Productions/Shutterstock.com; p. 24 right Dmitry
Kalinovsky/Shutterstock.com; p. 25 bottom SasPartout/Shutterstock.com; p. 28 Africa Studio/Shutterstock.com; All
craft photography Austen Photography

Cataloging-in-Publication Data
Names: Yates, Jane.
Title: Cool crafts with cardboard / Jane Yates.
Description: New York : Windmill Books, 2018. | Series: Don't throw it away...craft it! | Includes index.
Identifiers: ISBN 9781499482867 (pbk.) | ISBN 9781499482805 (library bound) | ISBN 9781499482614 (6 pack)
Subjects: LCSH: Paper work--Juvenile literature. | Paperboard--Juvenile literature. | Salvage (Waste, etc.)--Juvenile
literature. | Handicraft--Juvenile literature.
Classification: LCC TT870.Y38 2018 | DDC 745.54--dc23

Manufactured in the United States of America
CPSIA Compliance Information: Batch #BS17WM For Further Information contact: Rosen Publishing, New York, New York at 1-800-237-9932

CONTENTS

GETTING STARTED

To make great cardboard crafts, you need the right materials and a place where you can think and create. Your family may have a permanent space set up for crafting, or you can create one whenever you need it. You may already have many of the supplies shown here. Your family can buy anything else you need at a craft store or dollar store. Organize your supplies in boxes or plastic bins, and you will be ready to create in your makerspace.

A note about patterns

Many of the crafts in this book use patterns or **templates**. Trace the pattern, cut the pattern, and then place it on the material you want to cut out. You can either tape it in place and cut both the pattern and material, or trace around the pattern onto the material and then cut it out.

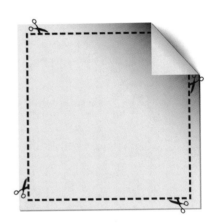

RECYCLABLES

You can make all of the crafts in this book with materials found around the house. Save recyclables (newspapers, used gift wrap, tissue paper, magazines, cardboard, flyers, junk mail, greeting cards, and more) to use in your craft projects. Use your imagination and have fun!

A note about measurements

Measurements are given in U.S. form with metric in parentheses. The metric conversion is rounded to the nearest whole number to make it easier to measure.

PAINT

RULER

SCISSORS

CARDBOARD TUBES

GLUE

SPONGE PAINTBRUSH

PERMANENT MARKERS

HAMMER

DUCT TAPE

RIBBON

DECORATIVE TAPE

PENCIL

TISSUE PAPER

CRAFT PAPER

PAPER NAPKINS

TECHNIQUES

Have fun while making your cardboard crafts! Be creative. Your craft projects do not have to look just like the ones in this book. You probably won't have the identical boxes and paper scraps around your home, so work with the materials you do have. Use the following techniques to create your cardboard crafts.

PAPER-MACHE GLUE

- Add equal amounts of white glue and water in a bowl. Mix the glue and water together with a spoon. If you have leftover glue, put it in a container with a lid and use it later. (An empty yogurt container works well.)

MAKING HOLES IN CARDBOARD

Some projects require holes to be made in cardboard. There are several methods.

- Use the tip of a pair of sharp scissors to create the hole. Push the tip of the scissors through the hole and then turn the scissors. If you use this method, always point the scissors away from yourself!

- Small holes — push a nail through the cardboard. Always point the nail away from yourself!

- Medium holes — start with the nail to make a small hole, then push a Phillips screwdriver through the small hole to make it larger.

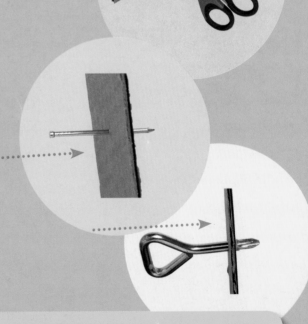

An adult should supervise whenever a project in this book requires using a hammer. Even then, everyone needs to be careful when using sharp instruments.

6

SADDLE STITCH

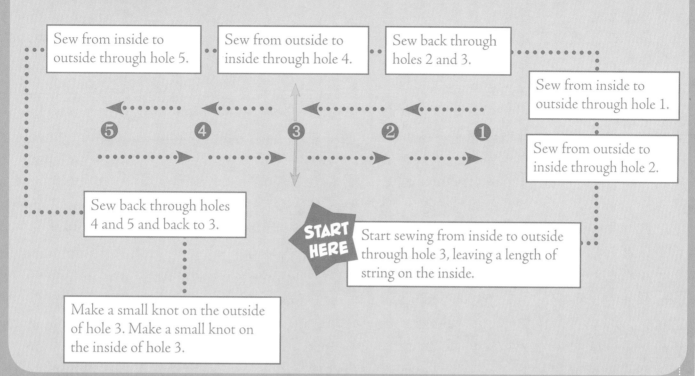

Sew from inside to outside through hole 5.

Sew from outside to inside through hole 4.

Sew back through holes 2 and 3.

Sew from inside to outside through hole 1.

⑤　④　③　②　①

Sew from outside to inside through hole 2.

Sew back through holes 4 and 5 and back to 3.

START HERE

Start sewing from inside to outside through hole 3, leaving a length of string on the inside.

Make a small knot on the outside of hole 3. Make a small knot on the inside of hole 3.

FOLDING CARDBOARD

Cardboard is easier to fold if you **score** the fold lines first:

- Place a ruler along the line you want to fold.
- Set a blunt tip* on the surface of the cardboard against the ruler.
- Press and pull the blunt tip along the ruler.
- Do not cut through the cardboard.
- Bend the cardboard at the indentation the blunt tip created.

*Scoring tool (you can use anything that has a blunt tip: a **retracted** ballpoint pen, dull pencil, screwdriver)

BE PREPARED

- Read through the instructions and make sure you have all the materials you need.
- Clean up when you are finished making your crafts. Put away your supplies for next time.

BE SAFE

- Ask for help when you need it.
- Ask for permission to borrow tools.
- Be careful when using scissors and needles.

DID YOU KNOW?

There are actually two types of material called "cardboard." One is flat cardboard, like a cereal box. The other is corrugated cardboard, which is two flat sheets with a wavy cardboard strip between them. Corrugated cardboard is stronger, but both types can be recycled many times.

Airplane

Inventors were making paper and cardboard airplanes like this one long before they could get real ones to fly.

1 Trace the airplane wing, tail, and body patterns found on page 31 onto a piece of cardboard. Cut out the body, tail, and wings using scissors.

2 Make slits where indicated with dotted lines on the pattern.

3 Color the plane pieces with paint or markers.

4 Decorate the plane with stripes of colorful tape and stick-on dots and stars (or make some to glue on). Slide the pieces into the slits cut on the body of the plane.

Make a small hole in the top of the plane, thread some string through the hole, and hang your airplane to a fixture in your room. It will fly whenever the breeze hits it.

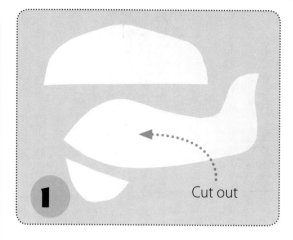

1 Cut out

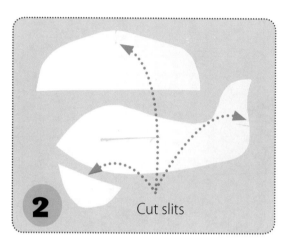

2 Cut slits

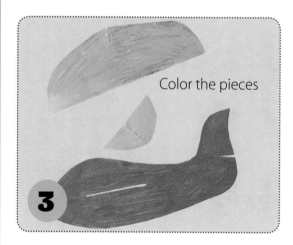

Color the pieces

3

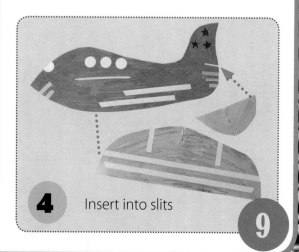

4 Insert into slits

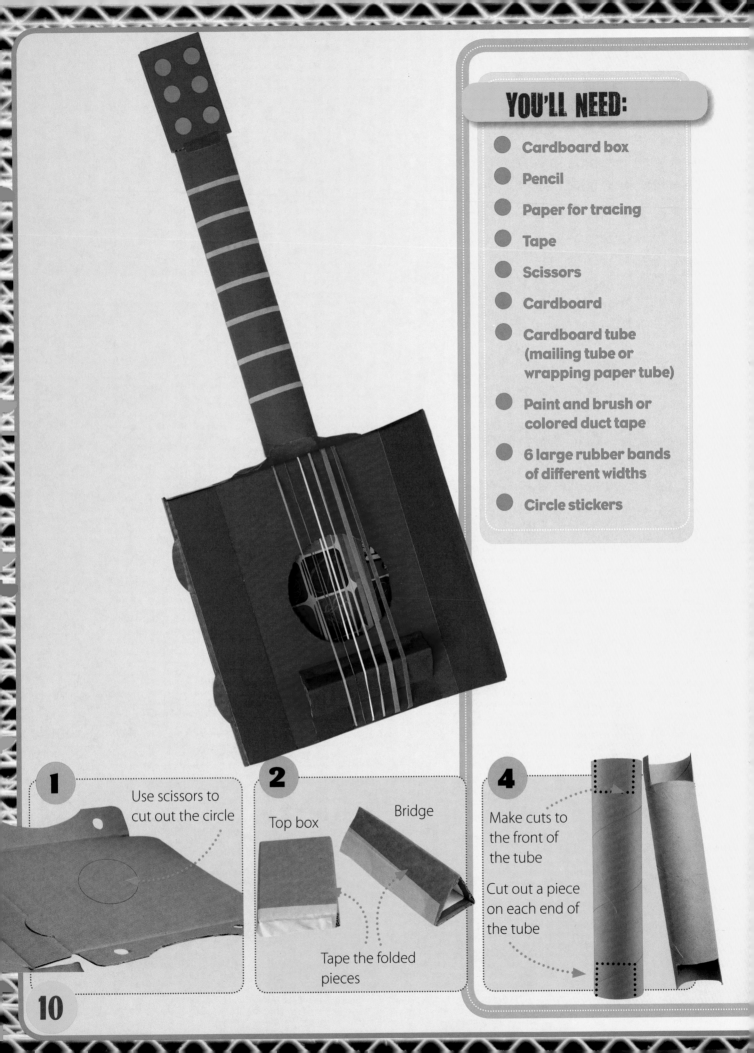

- Cardboard box
- Pencil
- Paper for tracing
- Tape
- Scissors
- Cardboard
- Cardboard tube (mailing tube or wrapping paper tube)
- Paint and brush or colored duct tape
- 6 large rubber bands of different widths
- Circle stickers

1

Use scissors to cut out the circle

2

Top box

Bridge

Tape the folded pieces

4

Make cuts to the front of the tube

Cut out a piece on each end of the tube

Guitar

This cardboard version of a guitar will make real sounds.

1 Unfold the cardboard box and lay it flat with the inside facing up. Trace the circle template on page 31 onto a piece of paper to create a pattern. Tape this pattern in the middle of the cardboard box. Trace around the pattern. Use scissors to cut out the circle.

2 Use the templates on page 31 to cut out two rectangular pieces of cardboard to make a bridge and top box. Fold the bridge piece twice to make a triangular shape and tape it. Fold the top box to make a box shape and tape it.

3 Decorate the cardboard box, the top box, the bridge, and the tube with paint or duct tape. Leave them to dry if you painted them.

4 Cut the tube as shown in the illustration.

5 Carefully stretch six large rubber bands of different widths over the box and position them over the hole. The different widths will create different sounds. Fold the box back together with the painted side out.

6 Fit the front of the tube under the cardboard box and tape it in place.

7 Tape the top box to the tube. Decorate the top box with circle stickers.

8 Pull the rubber bands up and slide the bridge under. Tape the box closed using duct tape.

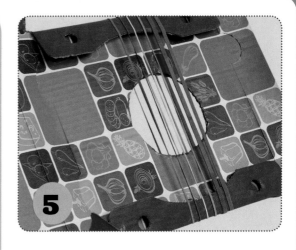

5

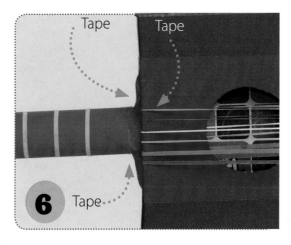

Tape   Tape

6 Tape

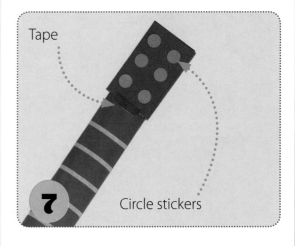

Tape

7 Circle stickers

8 Tape the box closed using duct tape

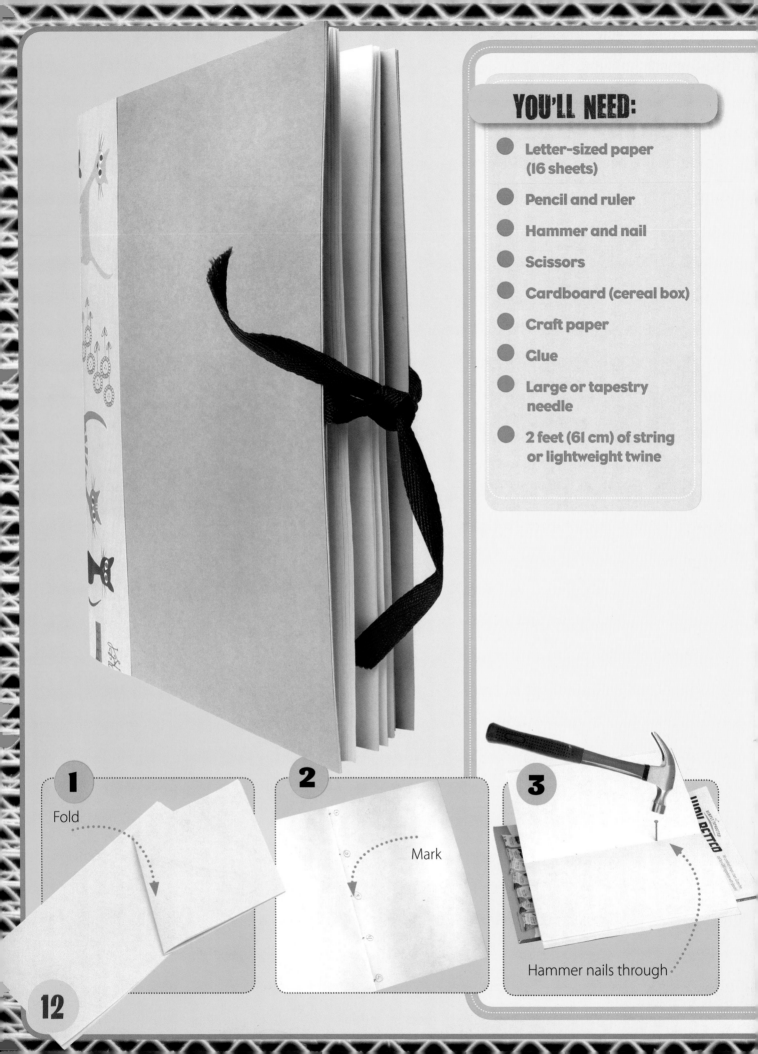

1 Fold

2 Mark

3 Hammer nails through

Notebook

Keep a journal or jot down craft ideas in a notebook that starts with a cereal box.

1 Fold the 16 pages of paper in half. Stack them one inside the other. Open to the middle of the stack.

2 With a pencil and ruler, make five evenly spaced marks along the fold.

3 Place a magazine or something similar under the paper. With a nail and hammer, make holes at the indicated spots on the paper.

4 Cut 9 x 11-inch (23 x 28-cm) pieces of cardboard and craft paper for the cover. Glue the craft paper to the cardboard. Cut a smaller piece of craft paper and glue down the center. Fold in half. Make five evenly spaced marks in the same places as the paper. Make holes as in step 3.

5 Put the paper inside the cover. Line up the holes. Use a large needle and string to sew book together with the saddle stitch. (See diagram on page 7.)

6 Cut two strips of craft paper 2½ inches (6 cm) wide and the same length as the cover.

7 Glue the first and last pages to the front and back inside covers. Glue the two strips on the edge of the inside covers.

You could make the pages out of paper bags. Flatten the paper bag. Use a piece of letter-sized paper as your template and cut out 16 sheets.

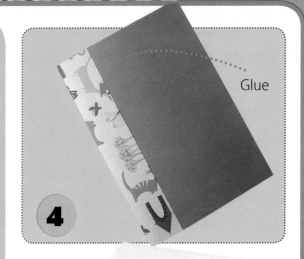

4 Glue

5 Sew together with the saddle stitch.

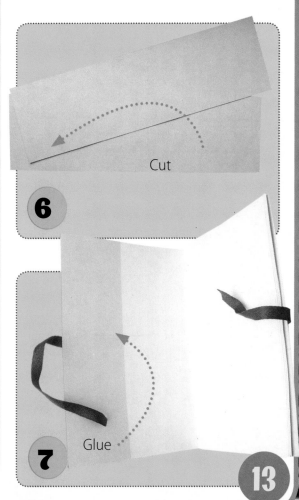

6 Cut

7 Glue

13

- Cereal box (or any other thin cardboard food box)
- Scissors
- Hole punch
- Glue and brush (double-sided tape also works)
- Tissue paper or old wrapping paper
- Ribbon

DID YOU KNOW?

The modern cereal box got its start with the Kellogg brothers of Michigan, who invented corn flakes in the 1890s. They packaged their cereal inside a cardboard box which was sealed in a wax paper bag. Today's cereal boxes are the reverse, with a plastic bag on the inside, but you can still see the bright red Kellogg's signature on boxes of the company's products.

Gift Bags

Turn cereal boxes into gift bags that are colorful and sturdy. Make a batch of bags for the holiday season!

1 Unfold the box. Start with pulling apart the side piece that is glued, then unfold the bottom. Optional: Make creases in the two side panels.

2 Cut the top off the box. Glue it back together with the inside now outside. Punch two holes at the top of each side.

3 Brush glue on one side and one side panel of the box. Cut a piece of paper bigger than one side of the box. Place the paper on the glue. Fold it over the top edge and bottom. Cut slits in the corners to help fold it over.

4 Cut two pieces of ribbon. Locate the holes you punched in the cardboard and punch through the glued-on paper.

5 Thread each end of the ribbon through the holes on one side of the box. Make two double knots on the inside parts of the ribbon. Repeat on the other side.

After making the basic bag, try variations. Write greetings on your bag with a marker. Add ribbons, glitter, stick-on stars, or other decorations. For holiday gifts, cut out images from greeting cards and glue them on. You can also paint or color a box with markers instead of covering it with paper.

1   Make crease

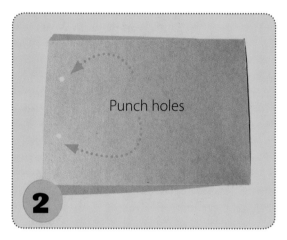

2   Punch holes

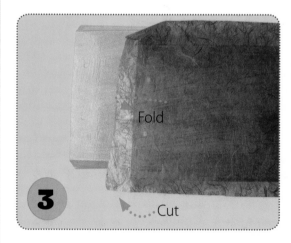

3   Fold   Cut

5   Knot

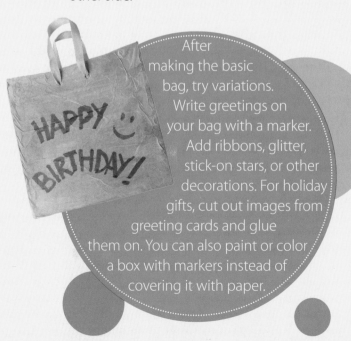

15

- Thick cardboard (for the frame)
- Pencil and ruler
- Scissors
- Paint in different colors
- Thin cardboard (for the mosaic)
- Paintbrush
- Paper
- Glue
- Tape

1

Cut two pieces

2

Draw a rectangle

3

Cut from the hole to each corner

Punch hole

Photo Frame

Make a colorful cardboard frame for a favorite photo. You could also frame a piece of artwork that you created.

1 Cut one piece of thick cardboard 8 x 10 inches (20 x 25 cm). Cut another piece slightly smaller and set it aside.

2 Use a pencil and ruler to mark 1¼ inches (3 cm) all around on the larger piece. Draw around the marks to draw the inner part of the frame.

3 Make a hole in the center and then cut out from that hole. Cut out the inner rectangle. Paint the frame white and leave to dry.

4 Cut thin cardboard into strips. Paint each one a different color and let it dry.

5 Using scissors cut the painted cardboard into various small shapes and sizes.

6 Trace the shape of the frame on a sheet of paper. Lay out the mosaic pieces and move them around until you are happy with the design.

7 Apply glue to the frame. Move a piece from the paper to the same position on the frame. Repeat until all the pieces are glued to the frame.

8 Put some glue into a small container. Add a few drops of water to the glue and mix together. Brush the glue over the frame to protect the mosaic pieces.

9 Tape your photo to the cardboard frame. Tape the smaller cardboard piece from step one to the back.

Another way to decorate your frame is with paint or the paper-mache technique.

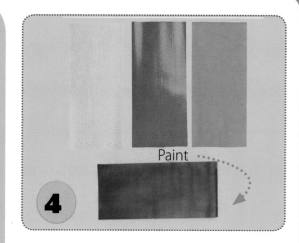

Paint

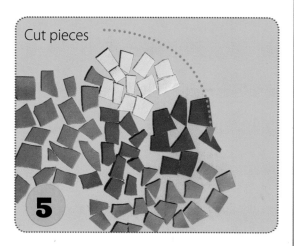

Cut pieces

5

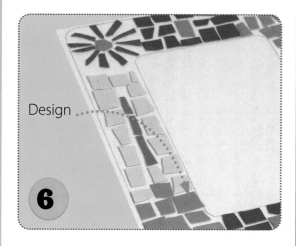

Design

6

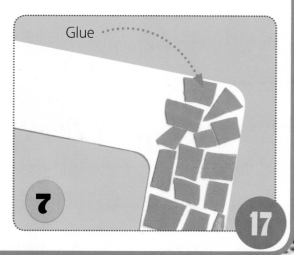

Glue

7

17

DID YOU KNOW?

Cardboard soaks up water and can jam recycling machines when it's soggy. Unless your recycling bin has a lid, try to put out cardboard only in dry weather.

1

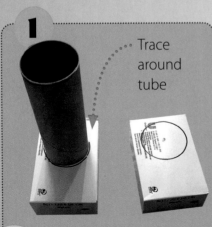

Trace around tube

2

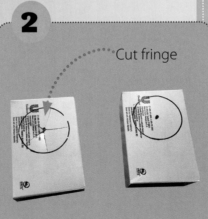

Cut fringe

3

Tape the tubes to the box

Sculpture

All kinds of cardboard boxes can be used to make sculptures. See what you have around the house and **adapt** these directions to create your own design.

1 Gather two soap boxes and a large cardboard tube. Cut the cardboard tube in half. Trace around the tubes onto the two soap boxes.

2 Punch a hole in the circle and then cut fringes around that hole to the circle you drew.

3 Glue or tape two cardboard tubes to the box.

4 Place a tube in the circle you made on each box and glue or tape it in place. Tape or glue the top of the legs to the bottom of a large cereal box.

5 Glue another tube to the top of the cereal box for a neck. Glue small boxes to the side of the box. Attach strips to these boxes for arms.

6 Cut a circle out of thick cardboard. Make a face using strips of cardboard. Shape cardboard into a mouth and eyes and glue on. Glue cardboard tubes all around the circle for hair.

7 Glue or tape the head to the cardboard tube attached to the cereal box. Make a cape out of a paper bag. Glue to the neck tube.

You can use regular glue for this project. Use blobs of it rather than a little drop. If you can use a low-temperature glue gun with an adult's help, that would work very well for this project as well.

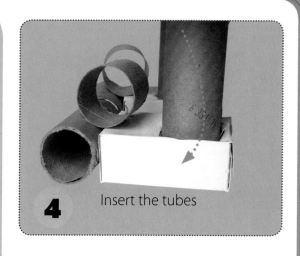
4 Insert the tubes

5

Make a face

Glue to neck

6

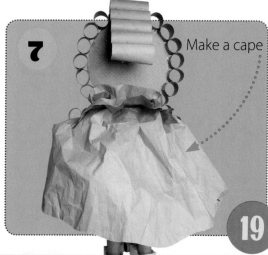
7 Make a cape

DID YOU KNOW?

Recycling just one ton (2,000 pounds or 907 kg) of cardboard saves 9 cubic yards (7 cubic meters) of landfill space.

1

Unfold the cereal box

2

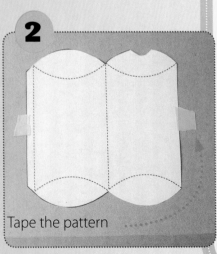

Tape the pattern

3

Cut

Pillow Box

Turn a cereal box inside out to make a pillow box. Use it for storage or a gift box.

1 Unfold a cereal box.

2 Trace the template on page 30 and cut it out. Tape it to the cereal box.

3 Cut around the template.

4 Cut around the dotted lines on the template, removing those sections. Tape to the cardboard piece again. Score along the edges of the template where the dotted lines are.

5 Fold the cardboard where the score marks are. Fold towards the printed side of the cardboard.

6 Decorate your box. You could color it with colored pencils, drawing many circles. You could also do it all one shade. Use pastels, markers, or colored pencils.

7 Use glue or double-sided tape to secure the long tab. If using glue, place a rubber band over it to hold it in place until the glue dries. Glue the bottom tabs together, fold one, put glue on it and fold the other one on top of the glue.

To make a gift box, cover it with tissue paper or wrapping paper using paper-mache glue. Once the gift's inside, fold the open end closed with the indented tab on top.

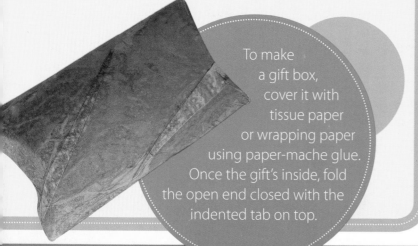

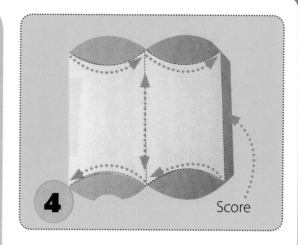

4 Score

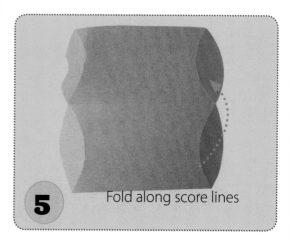

5 Fold along score lines

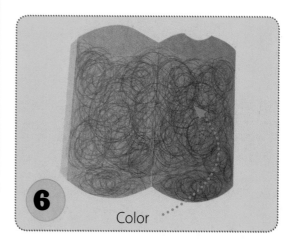

6 Color

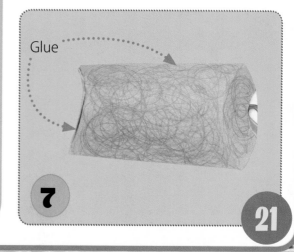

Glue

7

21

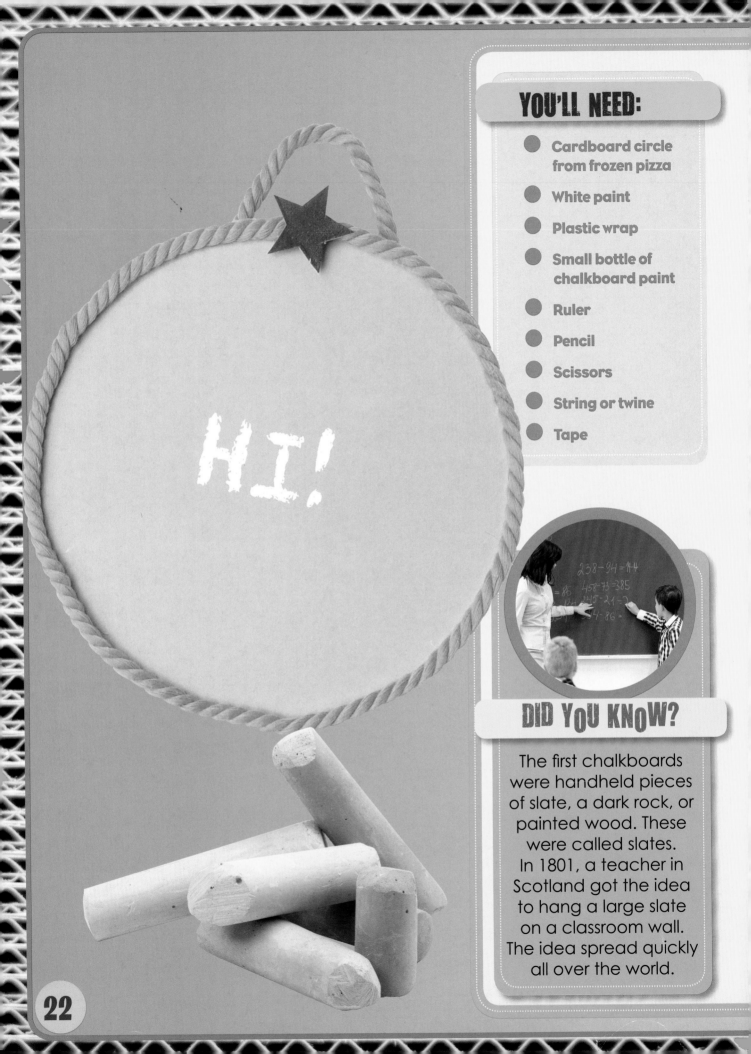

HI!

YOU'LL NEED:

- Cardboard circle from frozen pizza
- White paint
- Plastic wrap
- Small bottle of chalkboard paint
- Ruler
- Pencil
- Scissors
- String or twine
- Tape

DID YOU KNOW?

The first chalkboards were handheld pieces of slate, a dark rock, or painted wood. These were called slates. In 1801, a teacher in Scotland got the idea to hang a large slate on a classroom wall. The idea spread quickly all over the world.

22

Chalkboard

The first chalkboards were green or black. Thanks to special paint, you have lots of color choices for your cardboard craft.

1 Paint the cardboard circle with white paint. Paint the other side too (this is to keep the board from bending as the paint dries). Leave to dry on a piece of plastic wrap.

2 Paint one side with chalkboard paint. Leave to dry.

3 Cut a piece of string long enough to go around the board. Make a border of glue around the edge of the cardboard. Place the string into the glue and leave to dry.

4 Cut a 6-inch (15 cm) piece of string. Cut two pieces of tape. Tape the string to the back of the cardboard.

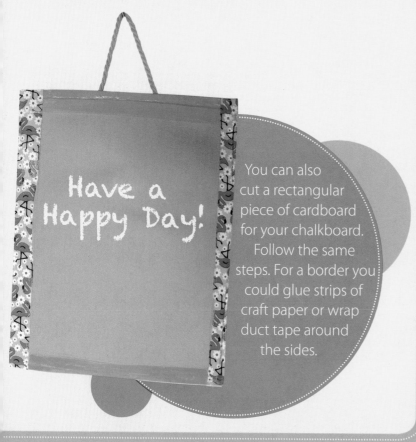

Have a Happy Day!

You can also cut a rectangular piece of cardboard for your chalkboard. Follow the same steps. For a border you could glue strips of craft paper or wrap duct tape around the sides.

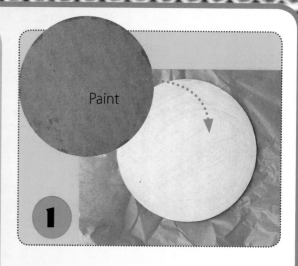

1 Paint

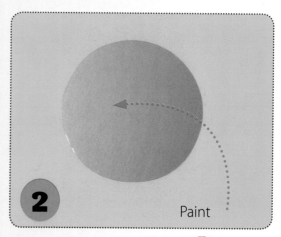

2 Paint

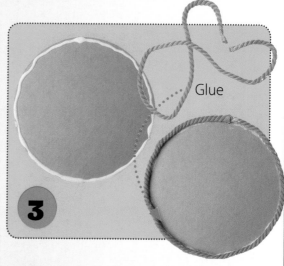

3 Glue

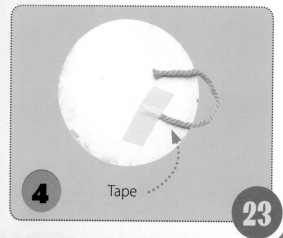

4 Tape

23

DID YOU KNOW?

Worldwide, there is more cardboard than any other kind of solid waste. In the United States, for example, about 90 percent of all products are shipped in a cardboard container. About 70 percent of that corrugated cardboard is recycled, but if everyone pitches in, that number can be improved.

Napkin Rings

Napkin rings are often used for fancy dinners, but they will look good on your family's everyday table too.

1 Use a pencil and ruler to mark equal sections on the paper towel tube. Cut into four pieces. Paint the pieces white.

2 Separate the layers of the napkin. Cut off one corner and then pull apart. Do the patterned layer and then the other two.

3 Cut away the **embossed** section of the napkin. Cut the plain pieces of napkin into squares. Cut the patterned piece into shapes.

4 Mix a container of paper-mache glue and cover one piece of the tube with it. Place squares of the plain napkin over the tube. Wrap it over each end. Add more paper-mache glue as needed. Dab more on with a brush.

5 Place the patterned shapes on top of the layer of plain napkins. Add more paper-mache glue. Be very gentle and dab it on top. Repeat steps to make a total of four napkin rings.

Make special napkin rings for holidays. Use holiday-themed paper or glue holiday-themed ornaments to the napkin ring such as a plastic spider for Halloween or hearts for Valentine's Day.

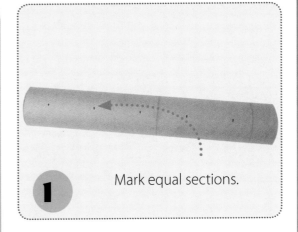

1 Mark equal sections.

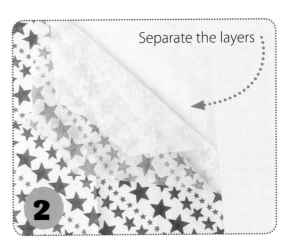

2 Separate the layers

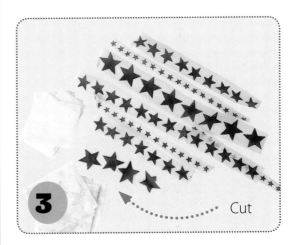

3 Cut

Add shape

5

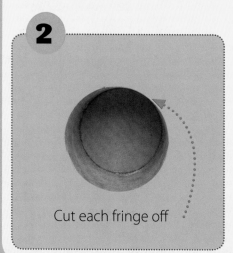

YOU'LL NEED:

- Round oatmeal container
- Scissors
- Craft paper
- Paper-mache glue
- Paper tubes
- Sponge brush

1

Cut fringes

2

Cut each fringe off

Art Organizer

Paper tubes and an oatmeal box can be turned into a handy holder for art or office supplies.

1 Cut the oatmeal container in half. Cut fringes down from the top.

2 Cut around the tube removing each fringe. Cut around the edge to smooth it out if it is uneven.

3 Cut some leftover craft paper pieces into strips. The length should be just longer than the tube.

4 Mix some paper-mache glue. Soak a strip for a minute. Remove the excess glue and place over the tube. Fold each end over the edges. Smooth out. Repeat until the tube is covered.

5 Cut a piece of craft paper slightly bigger than a tube. Brush glue on the plain side of the paper. Place the tube on top and wrap the paper around it. Tuck each end into the tube. Smooth the surface.

6 Repeat with the other three tubes. Leave to dry.

7 Place the tubes into the oatmeal container. The last one is a tight squeeze but it will fit. You can adjust the height of the tubes by shimmying them up.

3 Cut craft paper into strips

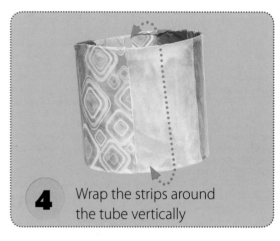
4 Wrap the strips around the tube vertically

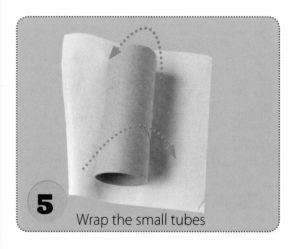
5 Wrap the small tubes

Tuck in
6

Put tubes in oatmeal container
7

DID YOU KNOW?

Kids have figured out so many ways to play with cardboard boxes that they were added to the National Toy Hall of Fame in 2005. Toddlers love hiding in them and so do cats! A big appliance box can become a playhouse or puppet theater. For older kids, shoe boxes can hold dioramas and larger boxes can be made into display boards for science projects.

3-D Animals

Cardboard 3-D animals make fun decorations for a party or holiday celebration.

1 Trace the pattern pieces on page 31 for the pig.

2 Use the pattern pieces to cut out each piece in thin cardboard. Cut a small tail out of a scrap piece of cardboard. Cut a slit in the end and curl it.

3 Cut the slits in each piece as marked by dotted lines.

4 Color each piece with crayons, pastels, or markers.

5 Glue the three circles for the nose together and then to the head. Place the nose just above the slit. Draw two eyes above the nose.

6 Insert the pieces together lining up the matching slits.

Make an owl too! The template is on page 30. Glue the eyes and beak to the smaller body shape. Glue the smaller body shape to the larger one. Attach the wings, ears, legs, and feet using the slits.

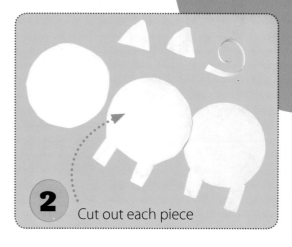

2 Cut out each piece

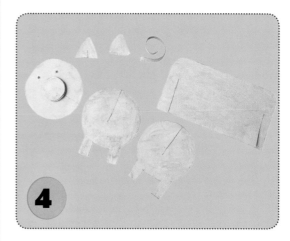

3 Cut the slits as shown

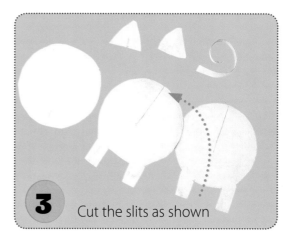

4

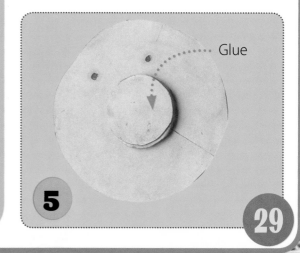

Glue

5

PATTERNS

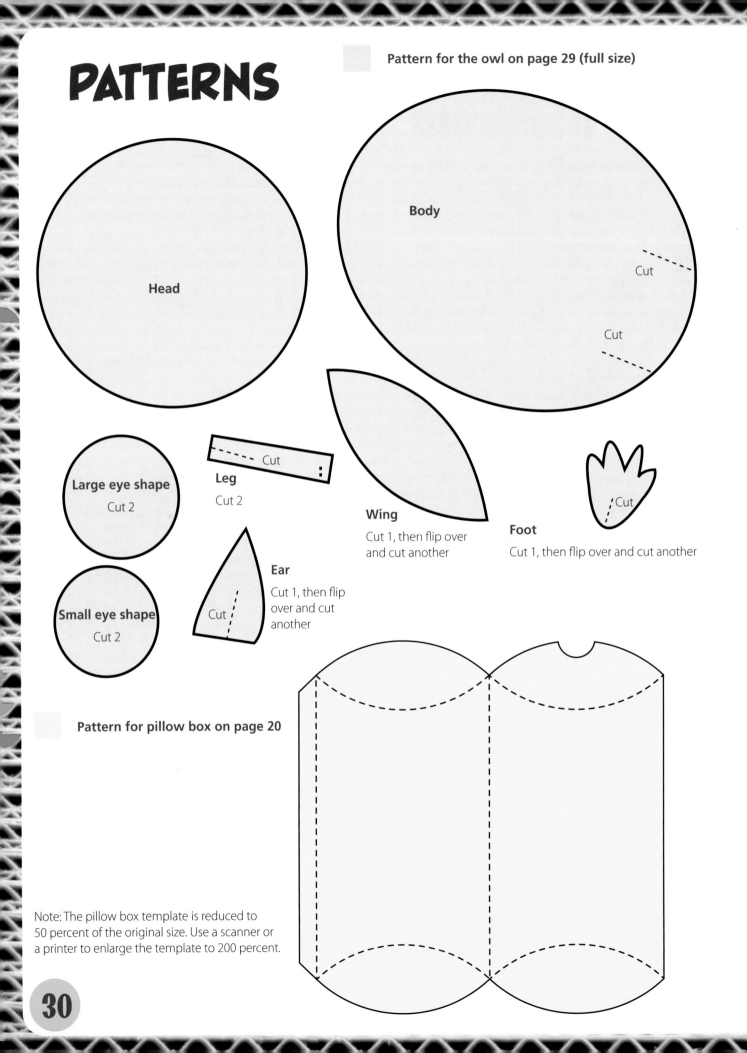

Pattern for the owl on page 29 (full size)

Head

Body

Cut

Cut

Large eye shape

Cut 2

Leg

Cut 2

Cut

Wing

Cut 1, then flip over and cut another

Foot

Cut 1, then flip over and cut another

Cut

Small eye shape

Cut 2

Ear

Cut 1, then flip over and cut another

Cut

Pattern for pillow box on page 20

Note: The pillow box template is reduced to 50 percent of the original size. Use a scanner or a printer to enlarge the template to 200 percent.

30

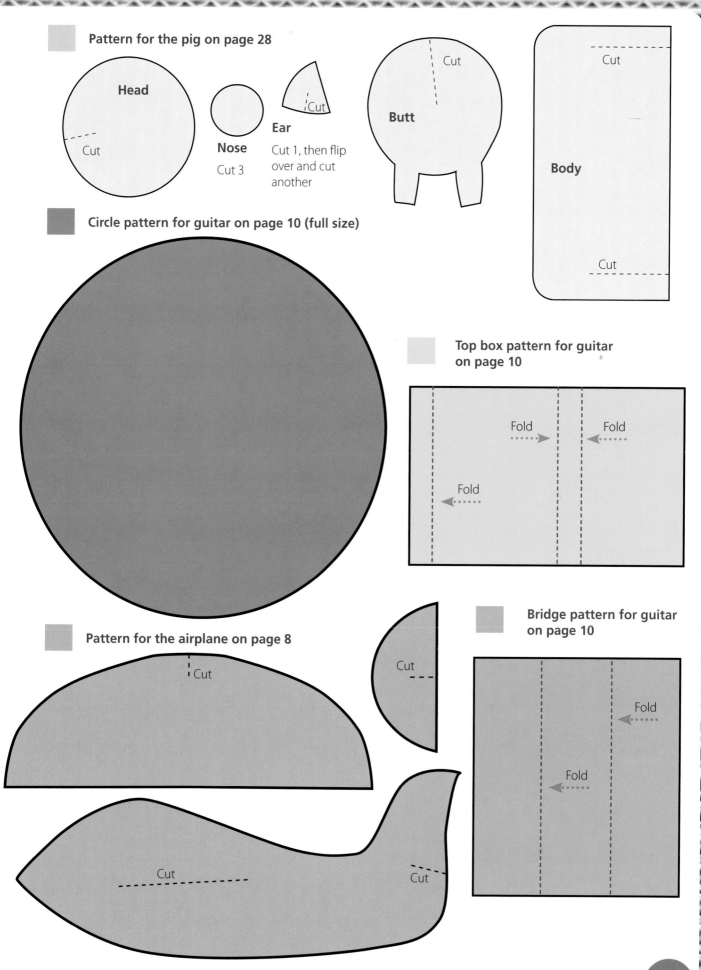

Pattern for the pig on page 28

Head

Cut

Nose

Cut 3

Ear

Cut

Cut 1, then flip over and cut another

Butt

Cut

Body

Cut

Cut

Circle pattern for guitar on page 10 (full size)

Top box pattern for guitar on page 10

Fold

Fold

Fold

Pattern for the airplane on page 8

Cut

Cut

Cut

Cut

Bridge pattern for guitar on page 10

Fold

Fold

Note: Templates for the pig, the airplane, the bridge and the top box for the guitar are reduced to 50 percent of the original size. Use a scanner or a printer to enlarge the template to 200 percent.

GLOSSARY

adapt Make changes so that something can be used in a new way.

embossed Decorated with a raised pattern.

retracted Pulled back.

score Mark with lines or grooves.

templates Shapes used as patterns.

FOR MORE INFORMATION

FURTHER READING

Hayes, Fiona. *51 Things to Make with Cardboard Tubes.* London: QEB Publishing, 2016.

Schwake, Susan. *3D Art Lab for Kids: 32 Hands-on Adventures in Sculpture and Mixed Media.* Beverly, MA: Quarry Books, 2013.

Ventura, Marne. *Big Book of Building: Duct Tape, Paper, Cardboard, and Recycled Projects to Blast Away Boredom.* North Mankato, MN: Capstone Press, 2015.

WEBSITES

For web resources related to the subject of this book, go to: **www.windmillbooks.com/weblinks** and select this book's title.

INDEX